Affection

By. Kenny Kay

Chapters:

I/ The Chemistry of Love.

II/ Soul Bond.

III/ Divine Love.

IV/ Yours Truly, …

V/ 2gether 4ever.

Chapter I :

The Chemistry of Love

Loving
the soul is
pure
Loving
the soul is
true love.

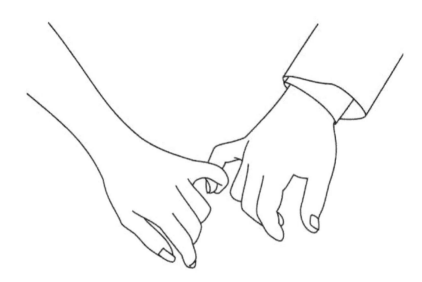

A glimpse of you
Took my sight away
A glimpse of you
Felt deep to the core of my countenance
A glimpse of you
Made me want to embrace the pain.

It's been a long time since

I felt the purity of your soul.

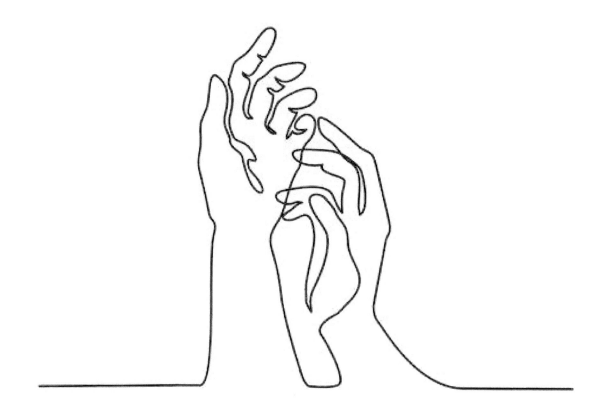

Dear Mom,
You're the light of my life
You made me see through the darkness
and
I've loved you with all my heart still I
love you until the end of times
my heart will always have a piece of you
that lies within.

Hold my hand
Let's leave it all behind us.

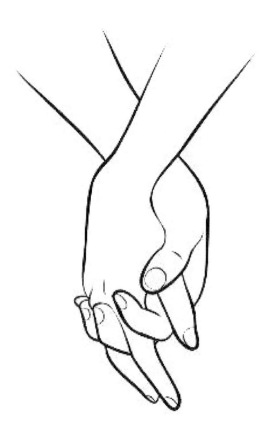

I shed one tear
I shed two tears
I shed three tears
I shed some more tears
I whipped every night because
I have lost the only person
I truly love in this world.

Hold me in your arms
    Put me under your spell.

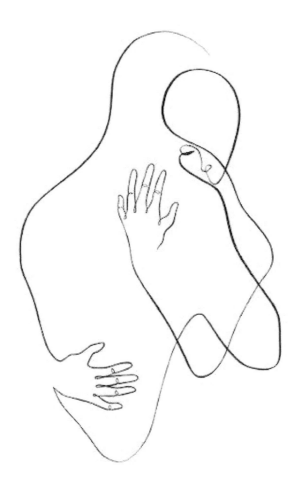

Sensual vibrations sequester
My feelings towards you and
I tremble and struggled to control it
So my skin flinched and my muscles tensed as
I waited for a mutual feeling from your side
while my eyes gently touched your skin,
yearning to see you every morning with a
smile upon your beautiful face,
I don't think I can live without you or to be
parted so painfully from you.

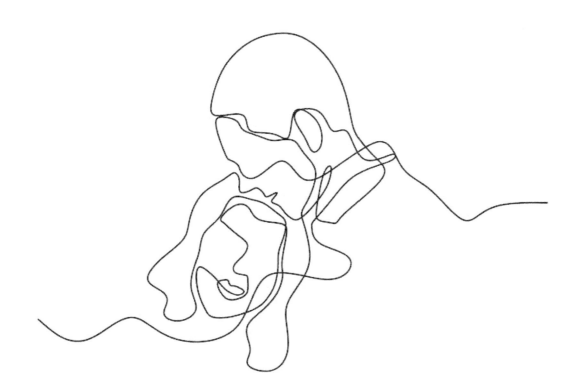

let me dive
into your heart so
I Can feel how warm It Is.

Let's make a vow that we may never break

Affection

Let's fulfil one another's needs with love

Let our needs be felt

Let me bury you deep inside to the core my love

so you may live forever in my heart.

I Long to hear your voice again
it brings warm vibrations to
my very ear.

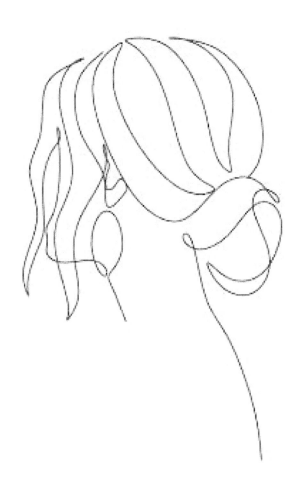

I have had a lucid dream last night

it felt so real that

I felt the touch of her hand

and the gaze of her eyes.

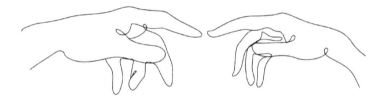

I Thought about kissing you...

and slowly feeling your lips and feeling your

 beautiful pale face with my finger

I Thought about kissing you...

While Honey's dripping across your lips and chin then

you licked it with your tongue

I Thought about kissing you...

In a car while it rains

I Thought about kissing you...

Under the rain while feeling

every drop of water on my skin

I Thought about kissing you...

Under a tree in the spring season.

I just want

to love you

like I never have…

There's magnet in her bones

it pulls me close to her

every time I lay my eyes on her.

Lonely in the dark cold night

Was Looking for warmth

But Nothing surround me but cold air

Cold as my very chest that's filled with pain.

Loving someone doesn't necessarily mean that

I want to make love to…

Love is intimacy and it make people

feel safe around each other.

Love is in the air

Love is all around us

Love is in every seed and every flower

Love is deep inside us if you look hard enough you will find it

Love is tender and soft as a newborn child's hands.

I need someone to hold me
and

tell me that

everything is going to be alright.

We met and I have enjoyed

your company

now we are nothing but

strangers.

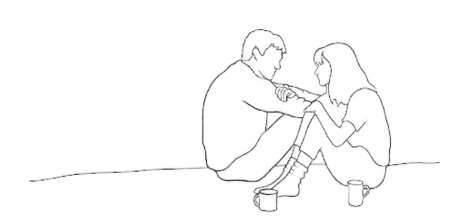

Am in love with every single

detail about her
Her eyes
Her smile
Her gaze
Her pink finger tips and
Her lips.

Self Love

Loving yourself

is your first step

achieving your goals.

Give me that
forever love
And
I will give you mine.

I got little diamonds in my soul
they sparkle in the darkest night.

A romance galore to
a beautiful woman and
a fine lady like yourself.

Together,
sipping tea in heaven
where we will last forever.

Today i woke up by the side of

the woman i love and

it's such a blessing knowing that

you're sharing your life with

someone you truly love.

I was in love once but
now i have forgotten how to love
Like if i was a caged bird
that had forgotten how to fly
But Still dream of the sky
and reaching the clouds .

Death doesn't mean the end or

that we will be parted so painfully from each other

Death means that we will be reunited in a better world.

I've given up on myself so many times but

you stood by my side and

held my hand so tight and

made me feel that am not alone.

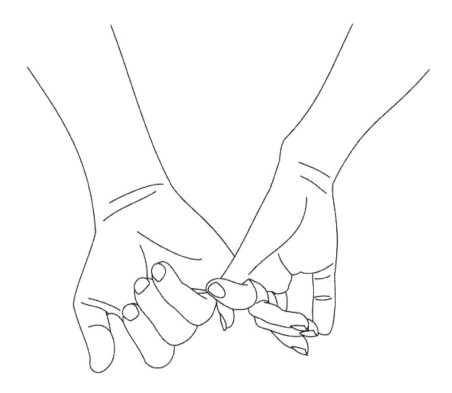

If you combine all the stars in

the universe they

still won't out shine

your beautiful soul.

In your beauty i learned how to write these words

You dance inside my mind

Where no one sees you

The moment i see your moves and

the way you dance that

very sight of you becomes this art.

Chapter II :
Soul Bond

I fell in love with the stars

And became

Fearless of the night.

Your smile

Is like

Magic to

My very eyes.

You carry the light in your soul

with tears in your eyes and

Love in your bones.

When i held you

I felt your aura surrounding me

It made me see the beauty of this world

It made me realize you are not

 just a beautiful soul but a home

Where i can be free of all burdens and sins

Where i can be held in your arms

Where i can be lost in your eyes.

If you cant be yourself

with someone

then that person isn't

 meant for you.

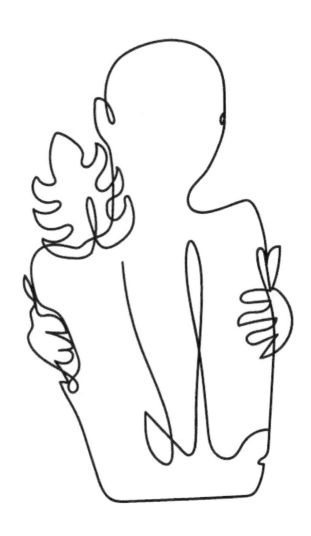

a message to the old me

You been through a lot I understand life can be

so dreadful sometimes

You are worth it

You are loved

Love yourself and will be a whole new person

Love yourself and you will find peace

Love yourself and you will find

the best version of yourself.

(The old me was in desperate need to hear this)

I want to restore

the feeling

The feeling I felt

when I fell for you

for the first time.

whether you love yourself and

be free or

hate yourself and

be a slave of the society.

writing poetry about

someone you love and

describe her with

every detail is like describing

the beauty of this world.

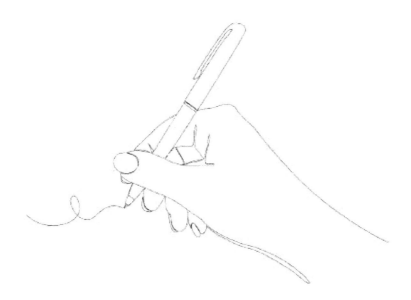

she's an angel that

has a smile that

brighten up the heavens.

I lose myself in words when I write about you

I keep writing like

I have way more to say

like I haven't said enough.

you are too good to be true

you are a blessing in this life and the after

you are a goddess of tenderness.

your smile is so stunning it
made my soul levitate
your eyes are so bright they
took my sight away.

your imperfections

are what makes you beautiful.

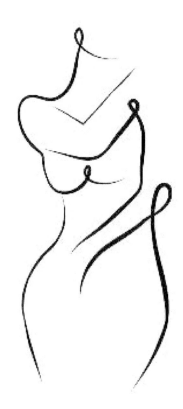

there's a wall surrounding her heart

I kept climbing trying to get inside but that

wall has gone taller

every time I climb higher.

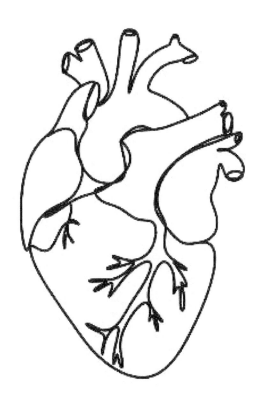

Caring about someone so much may

break your heart because

you will never know when that person is going to

turn his back on you like many others did.

I gave you my all and

loved you with all my heart and yet

You broke my heart into pieces.

looking at your eyes now

feels like a mirage.

there are no limits to feelings

we feel literally everything so deeply and that

may get us hurt one day.

her skin is soft as silk and

taste like cinnamon.

it was written in the stars That

scars were meant to be soaking all the light

It was written in the stars that love leave a black hole in our souls.

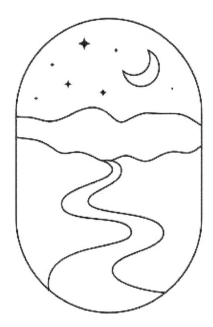

I whispered sweet words

in your ears and

you shivered beneath the sheets.

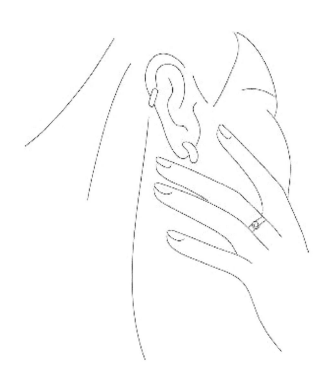

I gazed through her soul in awe

for how beautiful her soul is

that the light is breaking

through her lens.

Don't imprison your thoughts

Free your mind

Release your thoughts.

She's perfect

in so

many ways.

I miss you sometimes...

am not going to lie to you

To be honest

I miss you often

i miss you all the time

You're always on my mind.

am scared

scared of falling in love

scared of falling for someone that

will break my heart.

Lost Feelings

I really loved you with all my heart

 you was my first love I met you in a

dark time of my life and yet

 you managed to make things better for me

you brought the light into my life you made me feel

like am not alone

 you made feel loved I had nobody before you then

you came and brighten up

my whole life with your smile

 and then you changed for no reason maybe I was a fool

when I believed you really loved me or

maybe you just lost feelings

 it's hard to believe that losing feelings is a real thing but

I guess life can be full of surprises.

Chapter III :

Divine Love

Love can be bittersweet sometimes

if the love is real you will have to go

through thick and thin

through the bitter and the sweet.

you enchanted me with

your

Beautiful smile and

Pure soul.

I wish the time has stopped

the moment

I fell in love with you.

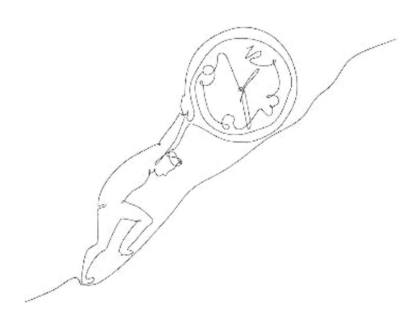

Sometimes I wish I died before

my mother but then I remembered

how much pain grief can cause.

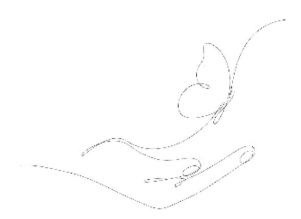

Longing for

your touch

longing for

your love.

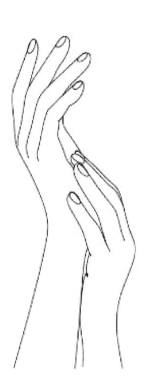

She told me to love her the way

I want to be loved

I crave no love if it ain't your love **I answered in complete serenity.**

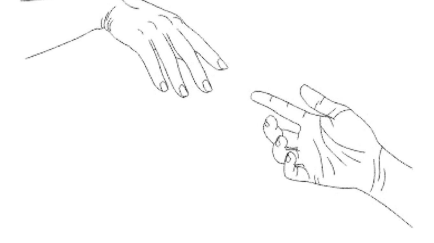

Her heart was meant

to be

handled with care

So fragile

That it might break like glass.

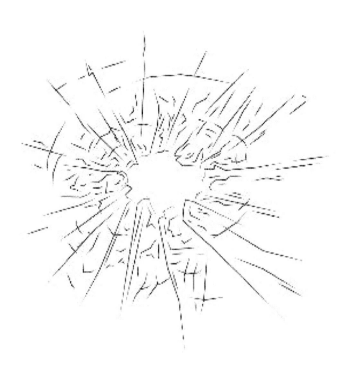

I feel like a caged bird because

am still stuck in the past and

it's keeping me from moving on.

You had me in my feelings and

I have been longing for your touch

Your affection

Your beautiful soul

Your lovely smile

Every detail about you is flawless...

If you ever felt lost without someone

that's not part of your life anymore

try to find the person you was

before that someone

became part of your life.

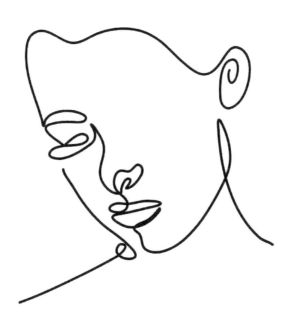

I don't dare you to change

I dare you to be yourself.

In my dreams

you're the most beautiful soul I have ever seen

In my dreams

you're the only one my eyes can see

In my dreams

you're the one my heart beats for

In my dreams

I feel butterflies in my stomach everytime I see you..

I say in my dreams

because is the only place I see you

I say in my dreams

Because is

the only place you exist.

If you don't feel butterflies

everytime you lay your eyes

on her beautiful face

she's not meant for you or

yours to keep

she's somebody else's.

I haven't seen your

naked body but

am in love with

your naked soul.

There was a wall around my heart

until you came and blew it away

like a typhoon and

left it vulnerable and open to be hurt.

Her Love has taught me

How to fly

with no wings

How to speak

with no tongue

How to see

with no eyes.

She has beautiful eyes even

when she cries

they twinkle like the stars.

All I need is...

your touch

All I need is...

your unconditional love

All I need is...

Hearing your sweet laughter

All I need is...

To be with you and hold your hand

All I need is...

your affection and care you used to give me

All I need is...

to go back in time to the first time we met.

All I need is...

the feeling I used to feel when am with you.

All I need is...you.

Scared of beautiful

Darling...

Your beauty scared
The fragments of my hearts
that are left in my chest

Your beauty scared
The unrequited feelings I have for you

Your beauty scared
 The most beautiful creatures in heavens

Your beauty scared
The goddess of love.

I love you in a way that

is no more healthy for me to love anymore

I love you in a way that

had me faded and jaded every night

I love you in a way that

made me question my existence

I love you in a way that

made me realize that life has no meaning without you

I love you in a way that

I became so lost in your eyes everytime I laid my eyes on you

I love you in a way

I never loved anyone else the same way I loved you.

Saying Goodbye...

Kissed her forehead then

felt her cheeks with my finger tips

her face was so cold

I kept feeling that cold in my fingers for days

that moment was never erased from

my memory and never will

it was the last time I saw her and

she wasn't even alive so

I could never tell her how much I love her.

After you left

I could still scent your smell in

the sheets and it continues to linger

all over the appartement it

made me miss you

every second of the day I spent at home.

I want my art to be felt

I want my art to be held

closer to your heart.

I see agony beyond your laughter

I see pain beyond your smile

I see beyond your silence

you are hurt but you're so quite and distant.

I just want to watch the sunset

While holding your hand.

Running away was never an option

Accept things as they are and

try to find a way to live with it is

the best solution

I ran away from my insecurities and

end up running in circles because

I was the problem

I should fix myself instead of running away.

Chapter IV :

Yours Truly,...

What is forever ?

it is something that has no end and

can be an infinite agony or infinite love but

what forever we really want

What forever we wish for...

Fresh Start

Sometimes you just have to close your eyes and

feel the touch of the sun on your skin then

take a deep breath

Can you feel it ?

Freedom... all burden is gone like it never was

The sound of birds chirping

The sound of waves crashing

It feels like...a fresh start.

I called you a home

I gave all of me

thinking you were the one

Thought it was a Forever Love but

I think nothing was meant to last forever.

- you were too good to be true

You were beautiful like a sunset

It take only a short period of time

never last forever still I spent that time

admiring your beauty until the night came and

your light was gone behind the horizon.

If they let you go

regardless how good you treated them

they were never worth it or worth to be with

let them go.

- as simple as it can be

Darling...

I wanted to give you my heart but

there is only pieces of it left.

Her eyes craves the very sight of the moon

Her ear craves "I love you" from someone that

brings her peace and comfort

He hands craves touching the pale face of a lover

Her feet craves feeling the sand.

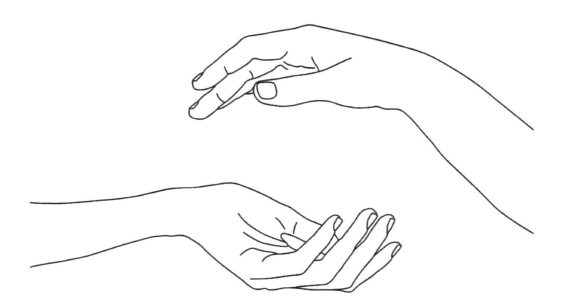

Her soul is her inner beauty that

ought to be felt and kept

far away from harm.

Don't expect anyone to stay

Everyone is temporary

Nothing was meant to last forever.

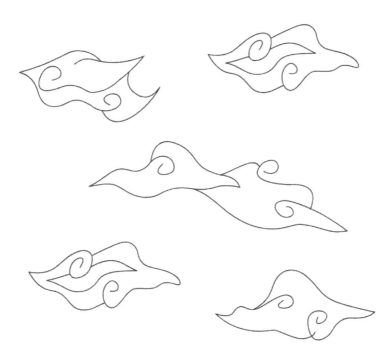

The roots of love have been getting

in too deep inside my heart that

I felt every word you spoke.

Family...

Love at it's pure form.

A Letter to Diana

January 31, Wednesday Night.

Am writing this letter to my beloved Diana to

tell you that you left scars in my heart and will forever be

bruised like any unloved thing in this world

loving you was never a phase or temporary

Loving you was a Forever and to die for kind of love

I hope that I have managed to capture my true feelings

 towards you in these words am writing and that you can feel

every letter that I am writing my love

- this won't be the only letter am sending

Sincerely yours, the person you once fell in love with.

I have been thinking about you all night

You are haunting me since the day I met you

I couldn't stop thinking about you,

vivid thoughts and unrequited feelings

You are the only one that I want

You are the only one that I need

love is so twisted that makes

 us do reckless things to

describe how we feel to each other.

This chapter of my life has come to an end

This chapter of my life was that part of my story

that felt real

felt real because I met you

felt real because you was the first one I fell in love with

so real that i questioned the existence of love

when I first saw you

So real that I felt your touch every time

I closed my eyes and thought of you

This chapter of my life has come to an end

The end that I never wanted it to come

The end that came with laughter and went with tears

I will forever love you

I will forever have a memory of

your passionate affection and care you gave me

will forever have a place for you in my heart

even if it's broken.

A Portrait...

I Made a portrait of a woman

 that I loved so much

I painted her with love and passion

painted her with

Black and grey

Yellow and brown

you could see

royalty and poverty in that portrait

Details made her look so real that

I almost believed she's in my room and

throwing that hypnotizing gaze at me so

 beautiful that made me feel the feeling

 I felt the first time I fell for her.

I Destroyed myself for you

I gave it all for you

was Fighting on to make things between us work

But you're so reckless that you didn't see my worth

I could see the stars glitter in your eyes

I could see agony drifting away from your smile and

tears sliding down your cheeks and

making there way to your lips

I Destroyed myself for you

I gave it all for you...I gave it all for you.

Losing control of my emotions

lost in a world of chaos and deception

then you came into my life

like a cold breeze and

turned it into perfection.

She showed me

how deep love can be

deep as the ocean

deep as her soul

deep as the universe.

there's a storm inside

everytime I think about her

A storm that my heart

can't handle anymore.

Reflections...

I was looking at my reflection in the mirror and

all I saw is

a body with no soul

Eyes with no single tear to drop

So I wonder if there's beauty behind

this mask am wearing

Is there a soul inside that's

longing to leave it's shell

Or is there another story to tell.

Ordinary Love

to fall in love with such a beautiful soul

as yours was never an ordinary love but

near to perfection

I can't say perfect because

you broke my heart at the end of it

I can't say perfect because

you chose not to love me back

I can't say perfect because

you were so reckless that you left

without saying goodbye.

Fragile heart

heart that aches when I see you

So tender as a butterfly's wings

so soft as a newborn child's hands

it will be broken at the end

Everyone with such heart will but

I still won't wish for a hard one that

doesn't feel a thing

I want to feel it all

The joy, The pain and The heartbreak.

Be colorful and

full of joy

Be fearless and

passionate about life.

She was poison to my very heart

Her sweet words and her bitter actions were a

woman's most powerful poison that a man can not handle

The way she said I love you

The way she look me in the eye and smile at me and

I have been lost in every action she makes and every word she says.

The sun sets in her eyes

So can the moon shine

before her smile.

Broken people

still deserve to be loved and

Broken hearts are

still capable of falling in love.

I said to myself that

the universe has a lot to offer

am still alive

still breathing

my heart still beating

so that's a sign not to give up.

Imagine what we could achieve

if we didnt spend our energy on

people who did nothing but break our hearts.

The time we spent together

The moments we had

are still living in us and

they will forever have a place in my heart

The heart that you broke and shattered into pieces.

Happiness has always been there for us

We just have to look closer among the stars.

Chapter V:

2gether 4ever

The sound of the waves crashing helps me

write with a clear head

I just close my eyes and

imagine a better world with

no pain and nothing but love

the true and honest type of love

the one that would never break

an innocent soul and gentle heart.

Sapphire eyes

Those sapphire eyes shine when she lies

They blue like the skies

that's not above us anymore

They blue like the ocean

that's so intense as a love galore.

Those sapphire eyes shine when she lies

Everytime she makes eye contact

I feel it in my heart there's a mortal pain

I still can't take my eyes away

 they driving me insane.

Someone else

I don't want to find you with anyone else.

You didn't just break my heart

you broke my soul

Caught between

 leaving it all behind and move on or

 keep thinking about the past and

 be trapped there forever.

There will not be another

who loves you the way I did

you were a romance that failed

I don't think you understand that

it changed something me

I don't think you understand that

losing you made me lose trust in

everyone around me.

Heartbeat

Put your hand on my chest and
feel this heart that beats for you
beats when I look at your eyes
beats when I see your smile
beats everytime I hear your voice.

Will write you love letters and

put them on the breakfast platter

along side roses that's how

I will show my love to you

every morning before I go to work.

you are the only one in this world that

saw the best in me

you are the only one in this world that

knew the real me.

I don't want to be cold hearted

it's the last thing I would ever want but

the weight I carry of hatred and agony made

my heart don't feel a thing and

I don't want you to feel that way so

I hope you don't go near hateful people so

 you can have a gentle and warm heart

like you always had.

you was the most beautiful soul

I have ever seen

you broke my soul into pieces and

it's the fragments that's making my heart bleed.

Darling you are in control of my emotions

I look into your eyes

I see my whole life before my eyes

before you I didn't believe in love

I never had anyone to give my heart to

Now I am feeling like my heart is leaving my body for

how hard he was beating

everytime I look into your hazel eyes

I felt that destiny wanted us together and

I know you felt it too

You are the love of my life and the apple of my eye

You are the first person I gave my heart to and

the only one that ever will.

am the same person you once fell in love with but

with a broken heart

The one you broke yourself and left it bleeding

you said without you I won't be breathing

but you never cared about a soul

Played with my heart like if it was a doll

no matter how much care and love I have shown

at the end you would say that all feelings are gone.

Affection

in an instant everything was gone

Gone with the wind

I don't know if it was all a dream

you took my heart and left like if it was yours to keep

you took my heart and left me with a hole in my chest

that turned into a black hole that soak all the pain in this world

in an instant everything was gone

Gone with the wind

Thought you were as faithful as an angel

but none of that is true I assume

I want to erase every memory I have of you

the good and bad all of it

Just like you never existed and that

I never met you in my life

your kind don't deserve to be loved but to be

broken just like you broke me

I still remember the first time you kissed me

and that makes me feel even worse knowing that

none of it was true.

Everything was gone

Gone with the wind

Every feeling

Every tear and

Every memory.

You look at me like you

haven't seen me in a long time

your eyes gaze through

my soul and witness all it's beauty

Like my aura made your soul

shine brighter than it was

there's a garden in her heart

 that's filled with rubble after I broke

 every wall surrounding it.

I was wrong all along

you weren't special

your love wasn't special

wasn't Special to make me

crave it the way I did

wasn't Special to make me

long for your touch the way i did

The only thing that really hurts is that

all you told me was fake and that

you didn't feel the same about me and

I believed everything you said and that broke me even more.

When the romance fails

Love will depart and with it

Only memories are left for us to live with

I wonder if your love was even worth cherishing

for it to become a memory.

Affection

will Return...

Cover Design by Kenny Kay

visit Kenny Kay on Social media

Kennykay4real

Milton Keynes UK
Ingram Content Group UK Ltd.
UKHW051427220224
438295UK00011B/324

9 798224 031740